My Hair Goes Up

HAIR POETICS

Poems, essays, and

ideas regarding the passage

of the CROWN Act

Leslie Rand Wilderson

Published by I am Here Pubs 2021
Cleveland, OH

ISBN Print 978-1-668-50988-3
ISBN Digital 294-0-162-48974-0

Cover design by Tanja Prokop and illustration by Vanja Dobre.

www.iamherepubs.com randmaison@gmail.com

The adaptation of this book into a theater production is intended.

AUTHOR'S NOTE

This poetic expression about naturally lofty hair is dedicated to Irma, Lillian, Jackie, Mary, Kimora, Trinity, Ariyah, Magnolia, Yaminah, Jaliya, Jaide, Katalina, Cali, Roteal, Amber, Orisa, Janisa, Debra, Judith, Phyllis, Pinky, Yamishe, Larry, Stanley, Timothy, Trevor, and everyone that has hair as full as clouds, which defies gravity to soar the beautiful skies with Saharan Doves. When we embrace our hair in its natural state, we have an unparalleled feeling of freedom.

Honoring George Perry Floyd Jr., a Human American who shared my geographic origin and nationality. His tragic death has forced a twenty-first-century examination and deconstruction of the systemic horrors that can arise from race categorization.

TABLE OF CONTENTS

I. HAIR POETICS

My Hair Goes Up

Up to the sky,
not down to the ground,
from atop my head ascends
magnificent hair
in a springy mound.
It makes me happy
to let it live free.
My hair walks tall
like me.

Original

My hair
is original;
it transcends its own path.
It makes one of a kind patterns
that change in a flash.
It may appear to be different,
but it's not quite unique.
Because
hair that goes up,
originated
on a great continent,
and its beauty
is omnipresent,
from Gambia
to Mozambique.

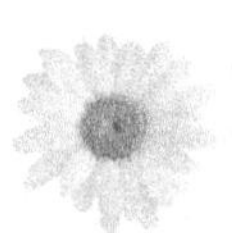

Splendor

I decorate my hair with flowers
and leaves.
It's as delicate and full
as the strongest of trees.
Its magnificent strength
protects my brain.
It's scented as sweet
as clouds after the rain.

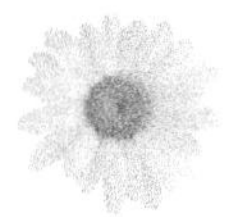

Naturally

Need I say that my hair exists
in a natural state, naturally.
Its phenomenal character exemplifies me,
just as I would
and should be.

When my hair is released
it soars like Saharan Doves.
On days that are breezy,
it is carefree and easy.
Its tiny tight coils symbolize love.

When my hair grows upward,
when it roams vertically,
I'm the best version of me you will see.

But the most important fact
about this sovereign entity,
which soars and roams naturally,
is its portrayal
of my liberty.

Natural: existing in or caused by nature not made or caused
by humankind.

II. THE DIALOGUE

A. Welcome, Dr. Wilderson; it is lovely to meet you finally. Thank you for engaging in this conversation.

L: Good morning America; thank you and likewise. I'm delighted to be here sharing my views.

A. Today, I wanted to discuss the dynamic book of poems and prose that you wrote called, *My Hair Goes Up*. I enjoyed reading it, and when I found out that this was your first book of this type, I had many questions for you.

L: Yes, writing about this topic and creating the poems was new to me. I usually write scientific and technical material, so having an opportunity to add a flowery voice to a topic that I have a lot of passion for was blissful. I especially loved creating the imagery in the short poems to convey the sentiment behind the work. It was refreshing to express my opinion stylistically in a fun and carefree way.

A. The poetic pieces really do evoke feelings of joy.

L. In a way, my intention was not to define but to describe how I feel about my hair and its impact on my world.

A. In your writing, you do not seem to be defending your hair, you describe it plainly as a natural occurrence. You also seem to describe your hair based on your own emotions and experience, and you leave open the opportunity for others to either relate or think about the way they experience their hair on their own terms. That was an uplifting stance.

L: Yes, the topic of hair is both personal and universal. I like that the writing developed that way. I cannot speak for anyone, but I decided to share my view and my positive hair experience. There are general sentiments regarding hair that goes up, and everyone has a deeply personal story. I have a happy hair story, and my love for my natural hair has grown deeper over the years despite the prevalence of hair weaves and other unnatural hairstyles in our society. In one poem, I expressed its delicateness and its strength in the same breath, which may seem paradoxical, but my hair strengthens my character when I refuse to acquiesce by accepting impractical hair standards. It is also delicate in a variety of ways, but in this narrative, I emphasize how the subject of hair is socially delicate.

A. You stated that you gave the piece a flowery voice. That seems like a lighthearted viewpoint to take with the profoundly dismal state of bias, intolerance, discrimination, and judgment that can surround the natural hair experience in America.

L: Ah, yes, those are often overarching reactions to my hair, but why shouldn't the topic itself be flowery. If one finds joy in natural things, one should not let those who harbor fear take that feeling away. Unfortunately, cultural identity discrimination seems to always loom in the shadows; although some may not be able to appreciate my right to vaunt the hair that ascends naturally from my scalp, my adoration for my natural hair doesn't have to change. Negative sentiments about my hair reflect poorly on people that hold prejudiced ideals.

I became aware incredibly early that when my hair was in its un-assimilated state that I was not portraying the integrated version of it that would receive compliments and praise; but learning that my hair was the target of overt discrimination and that it required laws to protect my freedom to show up with natural hair was disheartening. The fact that my hair is a target of discrimination cannot change how my natural hair makes me feel or my commitment to living naturally; it only deepens my resolve. In one of the poems, I also describe how my hair's magnificent strength protects my brain.

A. Yes, your metaphoric language in the poems was idyllic as well as thought-provoking. I sensed that you were referring to your mental state.

L: That's right, my hair in the natural state gives my mind an indescribable sense of peace. My natural hair contributes to my wholeness, and is essential for my overall well-being. It liberates me from the complicated rituals that altering it, covering it, or adding to it brings. The way I feel about my hair frees me from internalizing the negative messages surrounding me, which try to convince me that my hair must be changed into something unnatural to conform. And it just feels fantastic to be natural and dismiss the social construct designed to view my natural hair unfavorably. Natural hair is mood elevating. Among the many positive things it symbolizes, the greatest, by far, is power over your mind and body.

A: I noticed that you never mention how your hair may be perceived.

L: That is because I don't speculate on how it is perceived. In the context of discrimination, it has often been the target of hate. Yet that is not my focus, as Toni Morrison eluded that if someone has a problem, they should figure out why they have the problem. And they should figure out what they should do about it. It is not my responsibility or in the scope of this book to explain things from someone else's perspective. History tells us that the reason my right to life, liberty, and the pursuit of happiness is not respected stems from a long history of planned out prejudice and the exercise of power by one group of people over another. It seems clear that those acting from that premise need to find out why they continue to operate from that harrowing position, and they need to figure out how to change their behavior. Many great scholars have written about the psychological depths of racial division. The purpose of this book is to document that my hair, in its natural state, makes me feel happy and free and to reject the compulsion to mimic that which is not realistic for me. It also makes me happy to see the myriad of natural hair textures reflected by my family, friends, on city streets, on small and large screens, and around the world. I especially love seeing my childhood photos and realizing there was no other way I thought my hair should be at that time in my youth. I could not fathom that it was not just as it should be. Along the journey of writing this book, I used an image of my young self, one that I look at with extreme pride, to serve as the guardian of my words and justify why I should remain just as I was created. While it is lovely to fuss over, many things about myself deserve more focus and attention than my hair. And for the record, this is not a debate over aesthetics because all types of natural hair behold beauty. This narrative is about sentiment, equity, liberty, and peace.

A: I view this book as a fearless and resounding message that gives everyone with hair that goes up an opportunity and a responsibility to examine their thoughts and come to their conclusions about how they feel. This book also affirms the reasons to embrace natural hair with dignity and conviction.

L: Yes, it seems like a simple thing to do, and then the CROWN Act shows us the reality of the state of the centuries-old discrimination that caused irreparable psychological damage to a people by normalizing the alteration and repeated destruction of their natural hair.

III. RULE

In 2019,
a rule
to protect my hair was posed.
I ask for whom was this law passed,
and why my hair is opposed?

As everyone who sees me knows of
the vertical excursions
and adventurous journeys
on which my hair freely goes.

My hair is a natural occurrence,
a mutable feat,
a phenomenal treat,
to view.

So, the excitement and hype
to show my hair was unliked,
was a farcical thing to do.

yet,
by all reported accounts
and all communiqué,
the purported acts of
unkindness
and their malevolent defiance
made way for my hair's
Independence Day.

IV. THE CROWN ACT 1

(SB 188)

Create a Respectful and Open Workplace for Natural Hair

The CROWN Act is a California law, which prohibits discrimination based on hair texture and hairstyle by extending protection for both categories under the California Fair Employment and Housing Act (FEHA) and the California Education Code. The legislation was signed into law on July 3, 2019.

Professionalism was, and still is closely linked to European features and mannerisms, which entails that those who do not naturally fall into Eurocentric norms must alter their appearances, sometimes drastically and permanently, in order to be deemed professional. (Section 1. (b))

Despite great strides American society and laws have made to reverse the racist ideology that Black traits are inferior, hair remains a rampant source of racial discrimination with serious economic and health consequences, especially for Black individuals. (Section 1. (c))

Workplace dress code and grooming policies that prohibit natural hair, including afros, braids, twists, and locks, have a disparate impact on Black individuals as these policies are more likely to deter Black applicants and burden or punish Black employees than any other group. (Section 1. (d))

Federal courts accept that Title VII of the Civil Rights Act of 1964 prohibits discrimination based on race, and therefore, protects against discrimination against afros. However, courts did not understand that afros are not the only natural presentation of Black hair. Black hair can also be naturally presented in braids, twists, and locks. (Section 1. (e))

In a society in which hair has historically been one of many determining factors of a person's race, and whether they were a second-class citizen, hair remains a proxy for race. Therefore, hair discrimination targeting hairstyles associated with race is racial discrimination. (Section 1. (f))

Acting in accordance with the constitutional values of fairness, equity, and opportunity for all, the Legislature recognizes that continuing to enforce a Eurocentric image of professionalism through purportedly race-neutral grooming policies that are disparately impact Black individuals and exclude them from some workplaces is in direct opposition to equity and opportunity for all. (Section 1. (g))

The history of A merica is riddled with laws and societal norms that equate resplendent "blackness" and the beautiful physical traits such as melanin-rich skin tones, and hair full of life, as a badge of inferiority and subject to unequal treatment. (paraphrased) (Section 1. (a))

If you questioned whether the language used in the last paragraph was a part of the legislation, you would be correct in assuming that it was not a part of the CROWN Act as written. If it were written that way, with positive references to Black traits, it would have elevated its goal of addressing the fairness and opportunity issue that the law sought to deal with by incorporating respectful language, and thus, exhibiting respect for the humanity of persons possessing the referenced traits. If these physical traits were in any instance in the law referred to as beautiful or even as ordinary the way they are thought of by those who possess them, it could change perceptions. Instead, the law used language that did nothing to dispel the view that the targeted characteristics are inferior and not valued. The law as written makes fairness its basis for non-discrimination without humanizing the issue.

The actual section 1. (a) reads:

The history of America is riddled with laws and societal norms that equate "blackness" and the associated physical traits, for example, dark skin, kinky and curly hair to a badge of inferiority and subject to unequal treatment. (Section 1. (a))

The California law was the first legislation passed at the state level in the United States to prohibit discrimination based on hair texture and hairstyle. While an acknowledgment of the unjust, historical discrimination that has been inflicted upon the African diaspora is important, altering the language could have brought a greater sense of enlightenment to those engaged in prejudicial treatment. To use words affirming African characteristics as human characteristics may have garnered the reaction necessary for the evolution of moral sensibility. This would be a progressive step in a country with sordid history surrounding diversity, even if the enlightenment only occurred during law enforcement.

July 3rd, the day the California CROWN Act was signed into law, was declared National Crown Day, a Black Hair Independence Day. July 3rd is a day to proudly celebrate natural Black hair and Black hairstyles. Many expressed the sentiment that this law will further the cause to end the legality of being penalized for existing as oneself if you are Black.

Eventually, New York, New Jersey, Maryland, Virginia, Colorado, and Washington passed their CROWN legislation, and then the matter set off to the Capital.

On September 20, 2020, the United States House of Representatives passed the bill at the federal level. When approved by the Senate and the President, its protections would automat-ically ban hair discrimination in all 50 states.

The House of Representatives bill H.R. 116-525, Creating a Respectful and Open World for Natural Hair Act of 2020 or the CROWN Act of 2020, prohibits discrimination based on a person's hair texture or hairstyle if that style or texture is commonly associated with a particular race or national origin. Specifically, the bill prohibits this type of discrimination against those participating in federally assisted programs, housing programs, public accommodations, and employment. Persons shall not be deprived of equal rights under the law and shall not be subjected to prohibited practices based on their hair texture or style. The bill provides for enforcement procedures under the applicable laws.

In America, the survival of a people has been tied to their conforming to the dominating norms that were often unnatural for them and impossible to authentically emulate. Yet the adoption of the Eurocentric standard for hair styling is so ingrained in the culture that not even the Black is Beautiful movement of the 1960s and '70s could break the vicious cycle of blind conformity.

When armed with new legislative power, the question will be how can the victims of race-based hair discrimination become free from the oppression that they have internalized and that contributes to their current predicament of self-destruction? One day, those possessing dense, helically patterned hair will be fully protected against hair discrimination by the law of the land, and it will then be evident that it is purely a personal choice to oppress this freedom.

Creating a Respectful and Open World for Natural Hair

The official campaign of the CROWN Act is led by the CROWN Coalition, founded by Dove, National Urban League, Color of Change and Western Center of Law & Poverty. www.thecrownact.com

NATURAL
MELANIN
BEAUTIFUL
Alleles
Race
mutate Color geography
gradation character
free Love
MATTER RADIANT
EQUITY
BEAUTIFUL
HAIR
NATURAL
Venn
Intersection

V. VENN INTERSECTION

+ What if race as a human categorization is also meant to be a competition (v. race).
+ What if Black as the complete absorption of light, comparatively used emitted energy to enlighten all other colors on the spectrum.
+ What if the visual perception of color through long and short wavelengths of light was affected by the absorption of not only physical radiance but by the absorption of character.
+ What if DNA, the molecule determining the fundamental and distinctive characteristics or qualities of someone's development truly instructed a person's development and advanced their growth.
+ What if the origin of alleles and the evolution of love had a binary effect on equality by protecting quantitative and qualitative equity thereby ending race categorizations.
+ What if geographical origin, valuation, and appreciation were unifying agents that removed the human tendency to separate from each other based on human feature gradation.

+ What if the state of life energy as a distinction from physical matter became a significant energy source to transmute the matter of Black lives.

The point of this exercise in relating a collection of words and developing semantic statements is to show that when words are assigned meaning they develop into ideas and become fluid concepts acting as a function of their interpretation. Thus, removing labels from human existence would also remove invalid inferences and, therefore, eliminate the prevalence of *ex falso quodlibet*: from falsehood, anything follows and the *reductio ad absurdum*, which in this case is the reduction to the absurd consequences that exist from a long history of human divisions.

What if—then what?

VI. MATTERS

The sinister idea of race began in the eighteenth century and created attitudes about human differences. In the early construction of racial division, time was spent delineating the original five colored races into the Negroid, Australoid, Capoid, Mongoloid, and Caucasoid groups. In America, the race invention was transformed into human divisions for a labor system designed for capitalistic gains and had no valid biological necessity.

Matter is the physical substance of a human being that is distinct from mind and spirit. It occupies space, has volume, and is driven by spirit energy. A matter is also an affair or situation under consideration that has importance and significance. Besides matter and the degree of cellular variation that makes up the visual appearance, what is the human being? It would be easy to think that physical matter is the only consideration for human existence, given the emphasis placed on physicality. Even activities involving high-level cognition are subject to the influence of physical appearance. It seems interactions between humans are heavily influenced by physical appearance. The way the physical presence drives behavior during human interaction has a profound effect and is psychologically a matter that requires intense reprogramming.

Scientifically, it is a fact that even though all human physiological matter, derived from somatic cells is the same, a fraction of autosomal function is responsible for the spectrum of variation of inherited characteristics, specifically, the different gradations of the physical appearance of hair and skin, which are the basis for the fabricated race classifications. The concept of race is not biological, and therefore, racial categorizations do not have biological relevance in the function of the human body. Thus, the natural selection of pigment density in human skin results from differences in geographical solar exposure between human populations. This is explored in the study of molecular genetics of human pigmentation diversity. The research concluded that light skin color was a mutation created by a cross-over between two haplotypes in human populations from East Asia to the Americas and share a common origin[1].

In 2003, the thirteen-year-long Human Genome Project concluded after successfully sequencing the entire human genome, and we learned that there is no scientific or genetic basis for race[2]. Humans share the majority of our DNA, and the belief in the "races" and the structures of inequality that emerge from such beliefs are among the most damaging elements in the human experience both today and in the past (statement from the

---

[1] Canfield VA et al. "Molecular phylogeography of a human autosomal skin color locus under natural selection." G3 (Bethesda). 2013;3(11):2059–67.

[2] June 2000 White House Event. Retrieved from http://www.genome.gov/10001356/june-2000-white-house-event.

American Association of Physician Anthropologists, 27 March 2019). Since the cellular makeup between human beings is not appreciably different, when necessary, highlighting ancestral differences based on geographical origin is an ideal way to point out the genetic phenotypes responsible for the vast visual appearances found between different humans. America is a country that unites the world on its soil and can promote equality by disengaging references to gradation of skin pigment to describe humans. America has the opportunity to mitigate unethical practices that condone the separation of humans by cultural background because visual appearance and culture dynamics tend to obfuscate the quality of being human, which is essentially the only attribute that matters for equality.

The nomenclature, African American, adopted in 1988 to recognize its people's origin story came after many post-slavery references, including colored, negro, afro-American, and the colloquial term black. The change to the name African American intended to instill pride for the geographic origin of descendants of the enslaved in America. While it positively uplifted the group, the reference could not sufficiently change the stature of a majority of ancestral Africans in American society. African American became equivalent to Black as it pertained less to geographical ancestry and was systemically subverted to reference skin color. The more recently accepted adoption of the phrase "people of color" has become a softer sounding, socially accepted term used to refer to specific races. Essentially, its exploitation can render the term indistinguishable from the disparaging expression, colored, in its depiction. By and large, if a group of people must be grouped, the grouping should not be hierarchically structured or based on differences reflecting physical appearance, which have been a fundamental source of hierarchical separation. Socially, the reference to visual appearances like skin pigment has been manipulated to have negative connotations for some groups.

Again, the construction of race was the unnecessary evil that has caused the degradation of some humans based on the gradation of their human features. There is no noble benefit to humankind from constructing a system of division by gradation of features; there has been and only continues to be a grave detriment, destruction, and death. Since Africa is the origin of humanity and because humanity is the missing factor in the treatment of those with African ancestry, the people will one day cease to recognize the racial construct and decide only to acknowledge that they are human.

Nature is efficient. Furthermore, studying science and the intricate details of the efficient way life evolves is astounding. Coming to the striking realization that all living things are endowed with features essential to their survival not only explains the marvel of diverse physical traits, but this realization dispels the myths of superiority and inferiority. Nature finds a way to adapt and transcend conditions that threaten survival. To the great fortune of humans, we have evolved into a species that can thrive under almost any conditions except under the mental states of hate and division.

VII. THE AUTHOR

Dr. Leslie Rand Wilderson

What did I know of my hair before the world called it nappy?
What did I know of my hair before the world called it kinky?
What did I know of my hair before the world named it afro?

What did we know of our hair before the world assigned it meaning? At the beginning of our lives, we had no thoughts on the matter. As it became the subject of talk; and then a terrain that required a routine of intense navigation, we felt it merge from the fringes of our reality into a time-consuming challenge that caused us joy and pain.

In the sixties and seventies, it was easy to feel no particular way about my hair. There were free roaming afros all around me. Waking up with a smashed in natural and heading outside to play without giving it any thought was an acceptable thing to do. I had a big sister that took on the role of making it look nice and a father that took enormous pride in creating his famous top knot or two bum bums for me before school. My hair was cool. It was groomed with no reference to its physical appearance, and the grown-ups in my life referred to me as a deep young sister, which affirmed my sense of pride about my youthful intellect and "power to the people" appearance. I looked the part of a young Angela Davis, but more so, I was my mother's daughter, and my style was purely a reflection of her impression of the times.

As time went on, the transition from natural to physically altered hair gradually occurred. I am not sure when or why, but I know that it was during my high school years and of my own accord. It was my experiment. It was my dance with social curiosities, and I am sure that my family advised against it. Determined to get in on the action, and despite the existence of my perfectly healthy, luxuriantly bushy and beautifully thick, full head of hair, beauty shops entered my life with all their time-consuming, heat-inducing, hot combs and hair dryers.

Years later, I began to wonder if it was possible to consciously break the attraction that I had developed to an aesthetic that was mentally and physically destructive to emulate. After realizing the root cause for my unwitting proclivity to copy an unnatural hair appearance was from generations of assimilation, it became easy to break the hair straightening habit to portray a realistic version of myself. Especially when historically, incident after incident showed that people who shared hair characteristics like mine had experienced a broad range of antipathy from the group whose hair we felt compelled to imitate. It was apparent that I needed to restore myself to my natural self. I no longer affirmed the constructed hair beauty hierarchy that placed my magnificent mound of hair on the lowest level. The return to my natural appearance served to shield me from the state of oppression that my submission to conformity allowed. It also helped ward off the complicity that made me lose pride in my natural hair.

My normal appearance is melanin rich skin and dense, helically shaped hair genetically coded by my unique ancestry just as it was meant to be. And my confidence is the product of the balance and joy that comes from the way I care for and honor my mind and my body, and there are no outside influences that discourage me from embracing my natural gifts now.

VIII. TWO

I, too, am America's dream,
but not in the way I think.

Something feels new under the sun,
and it exists amidst the culture of oppression
that tries to prevent my dawn.

There is no shine for me on this side of the sun.
Yet the blinding darkness creates a glimmer of light,
to douse the shadow of a twisted reality
that seeps into my mind,
and dampens my synapses,
so I, too, hope that
I am America's dream.

When I am actually of a different star,
one that warms melanated bodies
with bright flames of
mind-expanding liberty,

a radiant light spectrum
cultivating free hair
to protect a free mind
on the top of a free body
standing dreamily beneath
a beautifully bright sun.

IX. SHORT TAKES

The word afro is a label assigned to hair,
based on geographic origin.
Afro may appear to be just a word,
and even a cool sounding word.
But when the natural phenomenon
of the emergence of hair from a follicle,
which is a factor common to all humans,
was defined in cultural terms,
that phenomenon opened the door
to more hierarchal separation.
Assigning hair a superfluous label
to set it apart
from the hair of others is problematic.
Hair is a natural phenomenon,
common to all human beings.
A process that categorizes hair by morphology
and separates humans by physical characteristics
is the foundation of discrimination.
Acknowledging variety can be a basis for respecting differences
but, there is also a deleterious line between
acknowledgment and categorization.

Equality is the foundation for respecting diversity,
therefore, all hair should be described by scientific analysis.
Hair traverses a broad spectrum of traits.
Regarding color,
eumelanin is a group of natural pigments
found in most organisms,
and darkly colored hair contains large amounts of eumelanin,
which exhibits a brownish-black color.
The physical appearance of hair texture
ranges by its strand density and shape.
The helically shaped, angular coil of a
strand of hair has a wide range of values.
A science-based system to quantify the varied helical values and
hair strand densities can develop products to care for all hair
types. The products can be uniformly labeled to accen-tuate
the formulation for the strand type, not to distinguish the
possessor of the strand type. [the de-emphasize hair movement]

Hair as art and fashion among some Americans has been
primarily based on aesthetic changes to the texture and length
of the natural hair.
It is not often that cinematographic images portray some women
without altered hair texture, and for those women, conforming
to this standard is usually written in the script, and methinks
thou dost not protest enough.
Just as the wardrobe that the actor dons in the scene is by design,
the hair choice in cinematic productions is most often not a nat-
ural choice unless it is called for by a period piece to reflect a time
when the trend was a natural hairstyle and, methinks thou dost
not protest enough.

Through imitation, he learns his earliest lessons—and there's no less pleasure felt in things imitated—Aristotle, Poetics.

The instinct of imitation is implanted in humans from
childhood. Otherwise, why would the victims of oppression
go to great lengths to emulate the hair
of those who oppress them?
Imitation by destruction and concealment of one's
naturally beautiful hair is a method to achieve an end,
if the result is aesthetic validation, not equality.
This is a road paved with duplicity.

What does it mean to want to imitate the one who has
deprived you of opportunity, prohibited you from obtaining
equitable services, and has felt threatened by your proximity?
This abnormal action silently validates the unfair and
unethical treatment that is present in all aspects of everyday
life, and such a simple gesture, the imitation of hair appearance
is a complex madness that says very loudly, "despite all that you
have done to harm me, I would look like you if I could."

Beneath my hair is a brain that wonders why I ever thought
any of the horrible ideas surrounding the contrived concrept of
race and the absurd judgments that accompany it ever
applied to me. Becoming unraced: the notion of being
unraced rejects human color references because being
human is relevant, and the only reference that matters
biologically and socially. Ending dehumanism (previously
known as racism) is the way forward.
"You want to fly; you've got to give up the shit that weighs you
down." -Toni Morrison

X. HUMAN AMERICANS

Every so often, in the quest for equality, justly so, and in the name of human rights, a certain group of Americans is compelled to implement a name change for themselves. Because in America, the convention to divide humans based on physical appearance is a norm; this group, also a diaspora seized from a distant land, once again chooses to be called by a new name. The new name symbolizes the evolved nature of their view of the antiquated system of oppressive domination that they live under, with its custom to deprive them of equal opportunities and divide them from other humans. The new name symbolizes a precise representation of their identity. The adoption of new nomenclature is also designed to distance them from the derogatory list of words they were called before and after gaining freedom from slavery. It symbolizes control over their lives and responsibility for solving the problems affecting their plight in a country whose colonial ancestors seized, transported, and enslaved them. It rejects the lesser status that the fabricated, race-based divisions inferred upon them.

The continual cries for inclusion and fair treatment remain

unresolved, so instead of making another call for inclusion, the phenomenal people that descended from a great continent in the Eastern Hemisphere, have chosen to adopt their original nomenclature. From this day on, they are referred to as Humans. And as Human Americans, the call for equality is well known to them. Therefore, they invite their fellow humans to denounce race and join them under this umbrella of unity.

The time has come to end the way humans define one another by the phenomenon of color perception, where the visual sensation of emittance or absorption of light on the skin's surface as perceived by the human eye becomes a derived source of discrimination. The cohort referred to as Human American is no longer willing to participate in the race. Their lives will not be defined by adjectives that describe the hues or textures of their physical features while humaneness is destroyed. Moreover, they recognize that human is the only label that truly represents them. This diaspora originated from the birthplace of human civiliza-tion. And their humanity has been tested for generations upon generations on this land and others, and they have prevailed with dignity as a solid representation of the human species. The quest for inclusion will lie with the groups that separate themselves from other humans based on physical traits and superficial differences.

XI. UN-RACED

Remove from the dictionary
one definition entry for the word race.
Remove the passage that defines race
as groupings of humans,
and the word race will still describe
the course of the sun or moon
through the celestial sky,
which shows majestic views of
the sea change in human interaction
and watches over the rise of nebulous clouds
that carry away the sojourn of a delusion.
Race will still define
the dash to discover harmony.
And it will still be the channel
of quiescent engagement
in a tide of altruistic goals

that humans can achieve
when the veiling dictionary entry
of race,
the one defining human division,
is removed from our consciousness.
Rid the world of archaic ilk so our hearts can beat
with the style and manner that allows
unfathomable liberation to create identities
based on affinity and feeling,
where there are no lanes or finish lines
to guide the exhibition of self-expression,
where the limits go beyond the sky
and humanity is fashioned by benevolence,
humankind is shaped by its journey of goodwill,
and where our power to navigate beyond
conviction is all owed to the omission of race.

XII. A GUIDE TO BECOMING HAIR BLASÉ

1. Realize that hair is just a tiny part of who you are.
2. If it has been a while since you've seen it in its natural state, become reacquainted.
3. Decide to accept your hair just as it is and know it is just as it is meant to be.
4. Be confident and embrace it as if there is no other option.
5. Touch, squeeze, and finger comb through it often.
6. Be seen wearing it in its many natural facets.
7. Go where you have not been in ways you have not been seen.
8. Realize that not conforming to society's unrealistic expectations of your hair is okay.
9. Show it love, and the world will follow.
10. Be free. Stay free.

    "I'm a believer in the power of knowledge and the ferocity of beauty, so from my point of view, your life is already artful —waiting, just waiting for you to make it art." -Toni Morrison

Say, what's up with the flat hair? Is it ill?
Has it lost its will to live?
Is there no water flowing to make it come alive?
Let me know if there's anything I can do.
I hope it gets better soon.

XIII. THE DAWN OF A GOOD HAIR DAY

The rediscovery of my natural hair occurred at age twenty-seven. I had not seen or thought about the texture of my natural hair since I was seven years old. Not only that, but I spent much time and exorbitant amounts of money making sure no one else did either. The momentous awakening happened during one extremely hot summer when my official dress code was swim gear and box braids. Over the summer months, the pool was my oasis. And by the end of the season, I had emerged with not only my water wings, but I also surfaced from the depths of the clear, blue pool water reacquainted with an old friend.

This virtuous friend, whom that I had avoided contact with for years and years, was now innocently standing right before me. I had been known to refer to this friend as the dreaded new growth, but within an instant of us coming face-to-face with each other for what seemed like the very first time, I was forced to acknowledge how cool she was. I decided it was time we got to know each other.

Over the next several months, the three inches of waviness that caught my attention in the early fall had turned into six inches of winter wool, and it impressed upon me a sense of delight to see the transformation of the texture of my hair. It, too, was delighted and could be seen basking in the sunlight and absorbing fresh air. My hair swayed, and it roamed its terrain creating stylistic patterns. And together, we became a force of nature that marked the dawn of a different sense of pride about my place in the world. I was showing up as my authentic self, and the world was in awe of me.

As my hair grew out and up, I referred to it as my experiment with natural hair, but soon I was forced to acknowledge my true feelings about what was happening to me. I decided that there was no way I could return to the time when I denied my hair its day in the light. What began as an experiment to allow a soft, curly mound of thick hair become free allowed me to feel one hundred percent myself. I was taken back to the days before I was seven, remembering when my mom worked her instinctive knack for creating the most fabulous styles a six-year-old in Harlem, New York, could have. I found myself nostalgically viewing photographs of our family in the days before I became naively mesmerized by my best friend's perm. That was a time before there was any telltale sign to warn me that my unquenchable thirst for silky, straight hair would last well into my second decade of life.

There was no warning label placed on the front of that fateful decision, and I was not prepared for the chemical hazards and mental chasm that I would fall deep into once I set out on the path to dismantle the inherently beautiful characteristics of my natural hair. I wondered in dismay at the irony I had lived, and I realized how unfree I was in my effort to live life with straight and free-flowing hair. The toxic concoction of chemicals and heat I used not only caused my hair to appear unhealthy most of the time, but that habit also diminished my ability to discern what was good for my hair. I showed myself that I could not make decisions about the fate of my hair objectively. I did not think critically during the years I engaged in the repeated destruction of a beautiful part of myself. Back then, I felt I needed my hair to look a certain way, which I achieved by adding chemicals and heat to it, and so rain or shine, I sought after the methods that made it bone straight, by any means necessary. After the emergence of my natural hair, I could no longer think of one rational argument to continue engaging in the activity of hair straightening. And I felt relieved by the sense of peace I had with my decision.

When I was officially considered "natural" and the last inch of treated hair was finally trimmed, I was overwhelmed by the acceptance and abundance of compliments I received. I showed up to work wearing my natural style without incident or fear of consequence. My ascendancy from the hair straightening abyss was triumphant. Over the years, I have realized that the societal influences that affect my life choices require continuous examination. I must be diligent in my decision-making and think critically about what I value and how I portray those values. My hair story was an internal revolution that I hope reverberates to affect the lives of others so they may one day feel the joy of a good hair day.

This story was told during an informal interview between the author and a good friend.

XIV. EQUATION

Allies are outsiders looking in.
The ally often defines himself as privileged.
The ally keeps a comfortable distance from me.
The ally makes a distinction between "us."
The ally recognizes our differences.
The ally is a part of the problem.

The fellow human is my equal.
The fellow human is aligned with me.
The fellow human appreciates our differences.
The fellow human views my issues proximal to their own
The fellow human internalizes my activism.
The fellow human is invested in evolving.
The fellow human is the solution.
Fellow humans are insiders, looking out.

- To Be Continued -

ABOUT THE AUTHOR

Dr. Leslie Rand Wilderson is a native of Queens, New York, residing in Cleveland, Ohio. After completing her formal doctoral education at Nova Southeastern University in Fort Lauderdale, Florida, she practiced Optometry for twenty-four years. She has published work on numerous topics in the health and science arena.

Dr. Wilderson has written a vibrant book using compositions and poetics about her hair to give a thoughtful perspective on social divisions based on human visual characteristics. Her goal with this book was to use a poetic voice to make a powerful, enriching statement about a vacillating and contentious part of the human story.